Welcome to
DUNNOTTAR CASTLE

It gives me great pleasure to welcome you to Dunnottar.
Though now approaching 100 years, my family have been
the Castle's custodians for only a relatively brief period
in its long and eventful history. However, ever since my
great-great-grandparents, the 1st Viscount and Viscountess
Cowdray bought the then crumbling ruins in 1919, our
guiding principle has been to maintain and preserve this
spectacular and important site for future generations.

Even as a regular visitor I am still struck by the drama of
its cliff-top situation and the palpable sense of its history,
and I hope it gives you as much enjoyment as it does to me
and the team who work so hard to look after it. Whether it
be exploring the Keep or Benholm's Lodgings, gazing out
of a gun loop and imagining Cromwell's besieging army,
or simply watching the magnificent sea-life, Dunnottar
encapsulates many of the best aspects of Scotland's
historical and natural heritage.

George Pearson

George Pearson

CONTENTS

Explore the Castle..4
Timeline..6

Explore Dunnottar Castle..............................**8-35**
The Location...10
The Gateway...11
The Inner Defences...................................12
The Pends...13
The Keep..14
The Storehouse...16
The Smithy..16
The Stables..17
Waterton's Lodging..................................18
The Chapel and Graveyard......................20
The Quadrangle..22
The West Range and Silver House.............24
The North Range and Drawing Room.......26
The East Range and Marischal Suite..........28
The Whigs' Vault.......................................30
The North and East Ranges......................32
Benholm's Lodging and The Fiddlehead....34

Historic Events at Dunnottar Castle......**36-49**
1297: William Wallace Massacres
        The English................................38
1562: Mary Queen of Scots Seeks Respite...39
1645: Montrose Lays Waste to Stonehaven.40
1651: The Honours of Scotland.................42
1651–52: Defending The Honours..............44
1685: Mistreatment of the Whigs...............46
1715: The 10th Earl Marischal
        Fights for the Jacobites....................48

Dunnotar as a Visitor Attraction...................50
Visiting Wildlife...52

EXPLORE THE CASTLE

1. Gateway
2. Benholm's Lodging
3. Pends
4. Keep
5. Storehouse
6. Smithy
7. Stables
8. Waterton's Lodging
9. Chapel
10. Graveyard
11. Quadrangle
12. Cistern
13. Silver House
14. Bowling Green
15. West Range
16. North Range
17. East Range
18. Marischal Suite
19. Whigs' Vault
20. Drawing Room
Toilets

TIMELINE

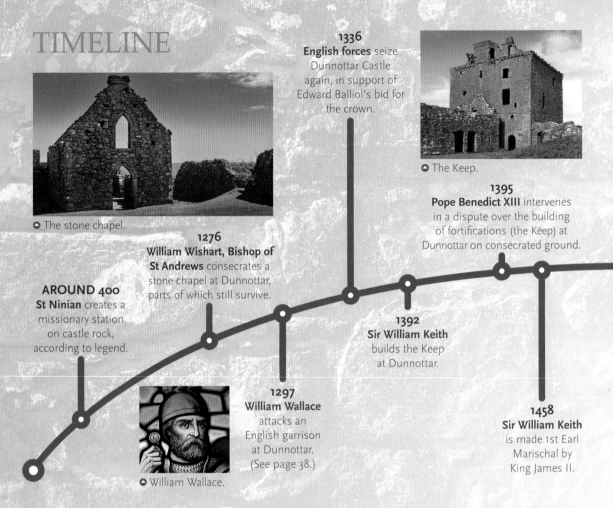

The stone chapel.

1336
English forces seize Dunnottar Castle again, in support of Edward Balliol's bid for the crown.

The Keep.

1395
Pope Benedict XIII intervenes in a dispute over the building of fortifications (the Keep) at Dunnottar on consecrated ground.

1276
William Wishart, Bishop of St Andrews consecrates a stone chapel at Dunnottar, parts of which still survive.

AROUND 400
St Ninian creates a missionary station on castle rock, according to legend.

1392
Sir William Keith builds the Keep at Dunnottar.

1297
William Wallace attacks an English garrison at Dunnottar. (See page 38.)

William Wallace.

1458
Sir William Keith is made 1st Earl Marischal by King James II.

THE KEITH FAMILY AND THE EARLS MARISCHAL

Marischal of Scotland was an important royal appointment that first appears in the records around 1180. At that time it was held by an East Lothian landowner named Hervey de Keith.

The Marischal's duties included presiding over court hearings and overseeing the royal stables, but as its name suggests it was mainly a military role. One example was Sir Robert Keith, who fought at Bannockburn in 1314, and was created Great Marischal by King Robert The Bruce.

The Marischal also had responsibility for care of the royal regalia, a significant duty when Cromwell invaded in the 1650s.

This was a hereditary post, and for over 500 years was passed down to members of the Keith family. They became progressively wealthier and more powerful, and in 1458 the Marischal was raised to an earldom, creating the title Earl Marischal.

Their association with Dunnottar began when Sir William Keith built the first stone castle here in the 1390s.

1639
William Keith, 7th Earl
declares allegiance to the
Covenanters, resisting
religious reforms of Charles I.
(See page 41.)

● The Whigs' Vault.

1685
**Over 160 Covenanters
and Whigs**
imprisoned in
terrible conditions at
Dunnottar.
(See pages 46.)

1919
**Lord and
Lady Cowdray**
purchase and
restore the castle.

1651–52
The Honours of Scotland held at
Dunnottar and smuggled out during
the ensuing siege. (See pages 42–45.)

1715–16
**George Keith,
10th Earl Marischal** is a key
figure in the failed Jacobite
Rising to overthrow King
George I. As a result, he
forfeits his title and castle.
(See page 48.)

1645
**James Graham,
1st Marquess of Montrose** lays
waste to Stonehaven and the barony
of Dunnottar. (See page 40.)

● George Keith,
5th Earl Marischal.

● George Keith,
10th Earl Marischal.

THE KEITH MARISCHALS OF DUNNOTTAR

There is disagreement between historians over the dates and identities of the Earls
Marischal – in particular the 2nd and 3rd Earls, and the 4th and 5th Earls. This list
should be read in that context.

Sir William Keith (d.1410) ....Built the first stone castle at Dunnottar
Sir Robert Keith (d.1430)
Sir William Keith (d.1463) ....Created 1st Earl Marischal (1458)
William Keith, 2nd Earl (d.1483)
William Keith, 3rd Earl (d.1527) ....Supported James III against barons' revolt (1488)
William Keith, 4th Earl (1501–81) ....Extremely wealthy; known as William o' the Tower
George Keith, 5th Earl (1553–1623) ....Arranged James VI's marriage to Anna of
Denmark (1589). Founded Marischal College,
Aberdeen (1593)

William Keith, 6th Earl (1585–1635)
William Keith, 7th Earl (1610–70) ....Covenanter whose Castle was used to jail
Covenanters (1685). Built the Marischal Suite
George Keith, 8th Earl (1614–94) ....Armed Dunnottar for William II and Mary II (1689)
William Keith, 9th Earl (1664–1712) ....Imprisoned in Edinburgh for Jacobitism (1708)
George Keith, 10th Earl (1692–1778) ....Major figure in the Jacobite Rising of 1715 who
lost his earldom and property as a result

EXPLORE
DUNNOTTAR CASTLE

THE LOCATION

Dunnottar Castle stands in one of Scotland's most dramatic locations, on a rocky headland jutting into the North Sea.

The surrounding region is known as the Mearns, a historic county to the east of the Grampian Mountains, just south of Stonehaven. For centuries, this area has provided the primary access route from central Scotland to the fertile plains of the Moray Firth and the north Highlands. Strategically positioned at the narrowest point between the mountains and the sea, Dunnottar acted as a fortified gateway which could be easily defended.

The rock on which the Castle stands is a conglomerate known as 'pudding stone', with large rocks and pebbles held in an immensely strong cementing matter, like raisins in a fruitcake. The rock was once linked to the mainland by a narrow strip of land, which has since disappeared, having been removed by hand to increase the defensive aspect of the Castle. Steps now lead to the only entranceway through the main gate.

The earliest records indicate that the castle rock was first occupied as early as the 5th century by a church which is associated with St Ninian. There is also evidence of Pictish habitation at Dunnicaer just north of the Castle.

In the 1390s the first stone castle was built by Sir William Keith, the Great Marischal of Scotland. The rock was now firmly established as a castle site and remained in the hands of the Keith family – later the Earls Marischal – throughout its active life.

THE GATEWAY

Visitors welcomed to Dunnottar Castle today can be thankful that they are not attempting to storm it.

With supreme natural defences on all other sides, only the landward side was vulnerable to attack. It was therefore designed to make hostile visitors feel as unwelcome as possible.

The arched Gateway (made smaller in the 1600s) would have been equipped with stout wooden doors. Inside it, a portcullis could be lowered as a further defensive barrier, and above it were ramparts from which arrows and other missiles could be rained on attackers.

Benholm's Lodging, to the right of the Gateway, strengthened the external defences. It bristles with three floors of wide-mouthed gun loops. This style of defence was introduced to Scotland in the 1520s, which suggests the building was added around then.

○ Looking up in Benholm's Lodging.

THE INNER DEFENCES

Any attacker lucky enough to survive the outer defences would now confront further hazards.

● The view from the guardroom behind the two-up, two-down gun loops.

The most obvious threat is directly ahead, where four gun loops are arranged in a very unusual two-up, two-down formation, directly facing the entrance. These are of the wide-mouthed type dating from the 1520s or later. The guardroom behind, where the gunners would be positioned, is carved into the rock. On the right hand side of the entranceway is a guardhouse, where troops could be stationed to repel invaders.

The guardhouse leads to the ground floor of Benholm's Lodging where a prison cell can be seen. The path turns left, overlooking the Castle Magazine, where gunpowder was stored. This would be an obvious target for attackers, but the low-lying path is surrounded by defensive positions from which they could be picked off.

The steps date from the restoration of the Castle in the 1920s. The original path would have been more difficult underfoot.

● A cannonball on display in Benholm's Lodging.

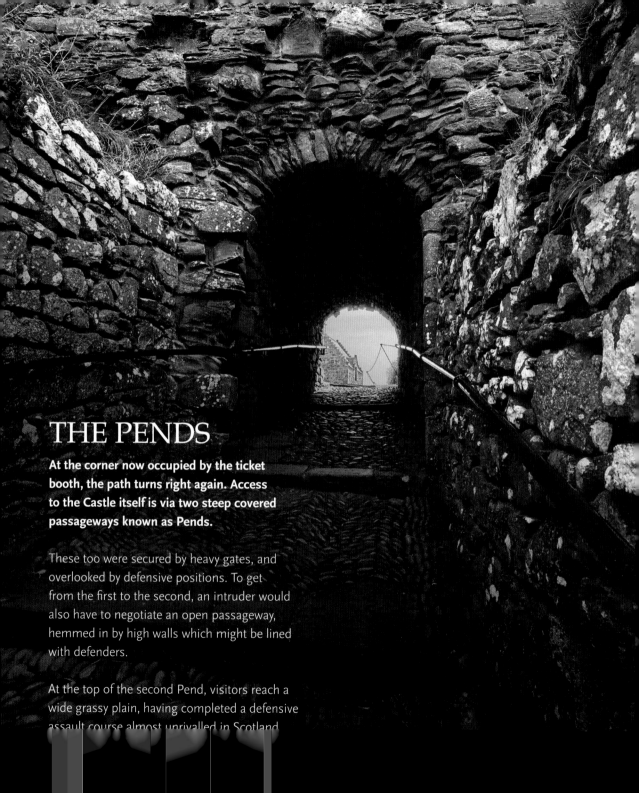

THE PENDS

At the corner now occupied by the ticket booth, the path turns right again. Access to the Castle itself is via two steep covered passageways known as Pends.

These too were secured by heavy gates, and overlooked by defensive positions. To get from the first to the second, an intruder would also have to negotiate an open passageway, hemmed in by high walls which might be lined with defenders.

At the top of the second Pend, visitors reach a wide grassy plain, having completed a defensive assault course almost unrivalled in Scotland.

○ Artist's impression of the Keep before the Storehouse was built next to it.

THE KEEP

The Keep was commissioned by Sir William Keith in the 1390s. It is still the most prominent building on the castle rock.

This is a fortified residence of a kind built throughout Scotland in late-medieval times, known as a tower house. Typically, a tower house had one room on each storey, but Sir William's Keep was L-shaped, allowing for a second room per floor.

A tower house often had an external timber staircase, leading to a main entrance at the first floor. This was a security feature, but the defences at Dunnottar made it unnecessary. Instead, the Keep has its entrance on the ground floor – though it was secured by a heavy door and a yett (iron gate). Above it is a niche where a religious statue was displayed.

A straight stone staircase (unusual for this period) leads from the entranceway to the first floor. The cavity under these stairs was a prison cell. The Earl Marischal was responsible for local justice, and the accused would have awaited trial here.

The kitchen is on the ground floor, but this was not the original kitchen – it was moved here from upstairs when the Storehouse was built.

The main room was the hall, on the first floor. This was the Keep's grandest room, a venue for meals and celebrations, trials and administrative business. It has good-sized windows and a large fireplace.

Next to it is the original kitchen, later converted to a private chamber. The kitchen fireplace is still in place: if you peer inside it you can see an oven at the left.

A spiral stair leads to the second and third floors. These would have held the master bedroom and other chambers. A small square 'caphouse' at the top gave access to a parapet walkway on which guards patrolled, adding yet again to the Castle's defences.

◗ Inside the upper floors of the Keep.

◗ The Keep and Storehouse.

◗ The ground floor and straight staircase.

THE STOREHOUSE

The building next to the Keep represents the first major expansion at Dunnottar.

When the Keep's kitchen was moved downstairs, vital storage space would have been lost. The Storehouse next to the Keep was built at that time, providing new storage for food and other commodities, and is still used as a storehouse today. It is a simple two-storey building with vaulted (arched) ceilings on the ground floor and living accommodation for service staff upstairs.

THE SMITHY

Metalworking was an essential function of an isolated castle with its own stables.

The ruined building next to the Storehouse has been identified as a Smithy, thanks to its large fireplace and chimney, and its position next to the stables. There would certainly have been a need for metalworking at the Castle, with many horses to shoe and many guns to load.

It was a mark of the Castle's importance that metalworking was carried out on the site. However, bringing iron to the Castle would have been challenging. It was transported here by boat, then hauled up the side of the rock by a winch.

○ The Storehouse, shown between the Smithy and the Keep.

○ The Stables.

○ The Smithy.

THE STABLES

As well as human residents, a dozen or so horses lived at the Castle.

Historically, horses were the primary mode of land travel for those who could afford them. At Dunnottar, a sturdy steed would also spare its owner the effort of getting to and from the Castle.

In medieval times, horses were generally smaller than they are today, and identified by function rather than breed. Horses kept at Dunnottar might have included destriers (relatively large warhorses), coursers (nimble steeds used for fighting and hunting) and palfreys (used for leisure riding and pageants). There would certainly also have been packhorses, used to carry goods up to the Castle.

The Stables had space for perhaps 12 horses, stores for their fodder and saddling, and accommodation for the grooms above. The grooms' quarters were reached by external stairs.

DID YOU KNOW?
Carvings found nearby at Dunnicaer indicate a Pictish settlement in this area around the 6th to 9th centuries. However, at least one of them is considered likely to be a 19th-century forgery.

WATERTON'S LODGING

The ruins of a comfortable two-storey house stand at the centre of the site.

Waterton's Lodging is named after Thomas Forbes, Laird of Waterton, a close associate of the 7th Earl Marischal. He attended meetings of the Covenanters at Dunnottar in the 1640s, and presumably lodged in this building. However, the style of the house suggests it was built well before that, around 1570–80.

The original residents may well have been the 4th Earl's eldest son, William, Master of Marischal, and his wife Elizabeth Hay. The 4th Earl was famously wealthy, but lived on in the Keep long after more comfortable lodgings had been added at Dunnottar. He may have built this house to allow his son and daughter-in-law (and himself) some privacy.

The building had two main rooms on the ground floor – one now turned into a garden, the other grassed over – and a similar layout upstairs. The two floors were linked by an attractive circular stair tower with a square caphouse at its top.

DID YOU KNOW?
An illustration of the Castle drawn around 1690 by the military engineer John Slezer shows a tall octagonal structure rising above Waterton's Lodging – a feature which also appears in other early illustrations. There is no record to explain what it is.

THE CHAPEL
AND GRAVEYARD

**The little church on the rock has been a site of
Christian worship since before the Castle was built.**

The Chapel was completed in its present form in the
1500s, but the original church was consecrated on
the castle rock in 1276. This makes it more than a
century older than the Keep – and according to
legend it replaced a much earlier chapel established
by St Ninian.

Earlier chapels would have been of wooden
construction, but some fabric survives from the
church of 1276, notably the small windows of the
south wall, with their pointed gothic arches.

The Chapel was orientated according to tradition, so
that its altar was at the east end. The main entrance is
in the west gable, rebuilt in the 1500s, with a gothic-
arched window above it, and above that a belfry.

The Chapel is now a charming and peaceful
space, but it was the scene of horrific violence in
1297, when, according to legend, William Wallace
massacred a large English army on this sacred spot
(see page 38).

Between the Chapel and the Stables lies an enclosure
which for many years was used to bury the dead.
Only one grave-marker survives. It states poignantly
that *'a bairn [child] of nyn years lyes here'* and gives
the date of death as 1685. This coincides with the
timing of the Whig prisoners being held at the Castle
so may be linked to that event (see page 46).

THE QUADRANGLE

Like most castles, Dunnottar was expanded and remodelled over time, in response to changing needs and fashions. The Quadrangle is a clear example of this.

It consists of three ranges of residential buildings created during later stages of the Castle's life. They are organised around three sides of a courtyard, with the Chapel forming the fourth side.

THE CISTERN

A water supply was essential for every castle, and Dunnottar's needs were met in an unusual way.

Near the centre of the Quadrangle is a large, circular enclosure full of water. This is not a well, fed by a natural spring, but the huge Cistern, 9.5m diameter and 7.6m deep, designed to collect and store rain water which seeped through the rock.

The nearest supply of running water is at St Ninian's Den, to the south of the Castle. Collecting water here and winching it up to the Castle would have been exhausting work, and highly perilous during a siege. Medieval people – including children – rarely drank water, partly because of the risk of disease. Instead, it would have been brewed into a weak ale, which purified it. An aperture on the east side of the cistern is thought to have been connected to the brewhouse.

THE WATER GATE

It was possible, if dangerous, to leave the castle rock via the Quadrangle.

At the north-west corner of the Quadrangle, a narrow archway passes between the West and North Ranges. This is the Water Gate, which gave access to a pathway down the rock to a little bay with a cave where boats could be moored. Following decades of erosion, the path is now too dangerous to use.

○ The West Range (left) and North Range (right), with the Water Gate at the point where they meet.

THE WEST RANGE AND SILVER HOUSE

This was the first part of the expansion that ultimately formed the Quadrangle. It was probably built by the 5th Earl Marischal in the 1580s. A wealthy, well travelled and highly cultured man, the Earl drew on influences from the European Renaissance when commissioning the building.

The West Range allowed for two key developments: more accommodation and the addition of a fashionable room called a gallery.

The attractive two-storey house at its southern end, the Silver House is probably so-called because it contained a strongroom for valuables. It may even have been used to store the Honours of Scotland (the crown jewels) in 1651–2.

Aside from this, the Silver House had a very important role: it held the staircase connecting the two storeys of the West Range.

At the back of the Silver House is a turret with a door at head height. This connected to the Bowling Green, the large grass area behind the West Range, via an external wooden stair (now gone).

○ The Silver House.

The ground floor of the West Range itself is an unusual arrangement of seven chambers, side by side, all virtually identical. Each has a door, two windows and a fireplace, but very limited living space. It is understood they were built as visitor accommodation and servants' quarters.

The northernmost of these chambers had its doorway blocked when the Water Gate was installed. The new doorway was created from the Bowling Green side.

On the first floor above six of the seven chambers was, the Gallery, a long, narrow room with large fireplaces and tall windows. An account of the 1700s describes it as *'curiously Ceiled with Oak after a very rich form'* – though sadly none of the decorated ceiling survives.

Galleries were fashionable in castles of this period. They were used for indoor leisure pursuits, including music and dancing – and for the display of paintings. This is the origin of the modern term 'art gallery'. A 'legionary tablet' from the Antonine Wall, constructed in Scotland by the Romans around AD 143, is recorded as having been displayed here.

At the north end of the Gallery was the small Retiring Room, where people could withdraw from the convivial atmosphere of the Gallery. It also connected with the Drawing Room in the North Range.

Some of the original off-white plasterwork survives around the windows of the Retiring Room. From the outside we can also see evidence of an external wooden balcony, reached from this room, which overlooked the bay.

◗ The turret at the back of the Silver House.

◗ The initials of Lord and Lady Cowdray, who restored the Castle in the 1920s, displayed on the upper south window of the Silver House.

THE NORTH RANGE AND DRAWING ROOM

The finest public rooms of the Quadrangle were housed in its central North Range.

The North Range was added soon after the West Range. Its ground floor contains storage cellars and the Great Kitchen (see page 32). The more prestigious rooms are upstairs, accessed via the impressive Great Stair.

The Dining Room was an expansive room with large windows on both sides and a great fireplace at the far end. It would have enabled the Earl to entertain on a grander scale than the hall in the Keep would have allowed.

East of the Dining Room is another Retiring Room with a latrine. This incorporated a gun loop looking out to sea, which was blocked by later additions.

West of the Dining Room is the Drawing Room, which was restored by Lady Cowdray in the 1920s. Her refurbishment was designed to commemorate the events of 1651–2, when Dunnottar Castle endured an eight-month siege to prevent the capture of the Honours of Scotland (the crown jewels) by Oliver Cromwell's army.

A stone carving above the fireplace pays tribute to George Ogilvy, Castle Governor, his wife Elizabeth Douglas and her kinswoman Anne Lindsay, who all played key roles in preserving the Honours.

The ceiling is also part of the 1920s refurbishment, elegantly panelled in Oregon pine and extensively embellished. It incorporates the gilded initials George Ogilvy and Anne Lindsay, Lord and Lady Cowdray, and the King and Queen then reigning, George V and Queen Mary.

Above the fireplace two relieving arches can be seen. These reduced structural pressure on the horizontal mantel. The doors on either side of it formerly led into the Gallery and Retiring Room in the West Range but are now blocked.

THE EAST RANGE AND MARISCHAL SUITE

The Quadrangle was completed by the addition of private chambers for the Earl and his Countess.

The Countess Suite, which occupies the upper floor of the East Range, was built by George, 5th Earl Marischal, around 1600.

Now in a very ruined state, it would once have been a very comfortable suite, comprising an outer receiving room, a more private bedroom and a closet or wardrobe (later used as a library). There are two windows overlooking the Quadrangle and at least five looking out to sea.

DID YOU KNOW?
This was clearly considered the Castle's most comfortable accommodation at the time of Charles II's visit in July 1650, for the young king slept in these chambers.

There was a secondary access to the Countess Suite, via an external stone stair at the east end of the Chapel, which presumably connected to her chambers via a timber gantry.

It would have been unusual for the Earl to build chambers for his wife and not for himself, but the adjoining Marischal Suite does appear to be later. However, the 5th Earl's second wife, Margaret Ogilvy, conducted a long affair with Sir Alexander Strachan of Thornton, and ultimately eloped with him, taking with her much of her cuckolded husband's wealth. This may help account for the unorthodox arrangement of sleeping quarters – and perhaps the back entrance!

The Marischal's Suite, which projects from the north-east corner of the Quadrangle, is thought to have been built by William, 7th Earl, in the 1640s. This was another handsome suite, comprising a private chamber and a bedroom with tall chimneys and superb sea views. It was, however, very exposed, and the windows were fitted with sliding external shutters to fend off stormy winds.

Remnants of the original plaster are still visible, and two fine pieces of stone carving survive, set into the west wall of the private chamber. One is a sundial, moved here from the lower Pend during the restoration of the Castle in the 1920s. The other, in its original position above the fireplace, shows the coats of arms of the 7th Earl and his wife, Countess Elisabeth Seaton. The date 1645 may mark the completion of the suite.

● George Keith, 5th Earl Marischal and his wife Margaret Ogilvy, who ultimately eloped with another man. The boy in the portrait is thought to be their grandson.

● Arms of William, 7th Earl Marischal, and his wife Countess Elizabeth Seton.

● A sundial, moved from its original position above the Pends.

THE WHIGS' VAULT

Below the Marischal Suite lies the scene of the most shameful episode in the history of Dunnottar Castle.

The vault beneath the Earl's private chambers was built for storage and defence. It slopes down toward the cliff edge, but could have been used to hold barrels of ale, sacks of grain or indeed military supplies. It is fitted with gun loops, allowing cannon to be fired out to sea. The large opening out to sea would originally been much smaller, but has increased in size as a result of stone being taken from the Castle prior to the restorations in the 1920s.

In 1685, however, this large space was used for an altogether darker purpose: as a prison for political prisoners. This was at the height of a period later known as The Killing Time, when torture and execution were widely used to exert royal authority against religious rebels known as Covenanters. (You can read more about this on pages 46–7.)

One hundred and sixty-seven prisoners were confined in the Whigs' Vault, and many were held here from 24 May until the end of July, with minimal food, water, privacy and sanitation.

About 40 prisoners were eventually removed to other chambers in the castle, including the Thief's Hole beneath the Whigs' Vault, which was presumably built as a prison cell. This may have alleviated some of the overcrowding, but prisoners in the lower chamber found themselves directly below the drain from the crowded vault above.

● The Thief's Hole.

THE NORTH AND EAST RANGES:

GROUND FLOOR

Aside from the notorious vault, the ground floor of the Quadrangle was used for conventional purposes: to house storage cellars and facilities to serve the needs of the household. Their vaulted ceilings helped support the grander rooms above.

THE NORTH RANGE

The rooms below the Drawing Room and Dining Room were used to house the Great Kitchen and storage chambers.

When the Quadrangle was built, the main residential focus of the Castle shifted, and the associated services had to move too. Above all, a good-sized kitchen was required.

This was built directly below the grand Dining Room, and provided cooking facilities on a grand scale. The huge fireplace arch is 3m deep and almost 4m wide with a correspondingly huge chimney, and within it two domed ovens can be seen.

Just outside the fireplace is a slop drain, for disposing of waste, and next to it a very worn stone trough, which might have been used for cleaning or mixing ingredients. Finished dishes were passed through the serving hatch to be carried upstairs to the Dining Room.

Food, wine, ale and other supplies had to be kept close to the kitchen, and the north range's ground floor is completed by three storage cellars. Two of them are still used for storage today.

● A vaulted corridor leading to the Whig's Vault.

● A stone basin, still in its original position near the kitchen drain.

◔ The Kitchen.

THE EAST RANGE

Beneath the Countess Suite two essential products were made: bread and ale.

Across the entrance lobby from the kitchen lies a sequence of three rooms. The first is another storage cellar, perhaps used for flour and barley. Beyond this is the Brewery.

A pipeline connected the Cistern to the Brewery, where a simple brewing process transformed it into weak ale, allowing all residents of the Castle to enjoy safe refreshment, and just a little intoxication. Part of the stonework used in the brewing process remains today.

Beyond the Brewery is a large Bakehouse, where bread was produced. Its massive oven can be seen from outside the building, just beyond the Chapel.

DID YOU KNOW?

Many people have reported uncanny feelings in this part of the Castle. Sightings of various ghosts have been reported, including; a sad-looking woman wearing green plaid (a traditional chequered fabric); a Scandinavian-looking soldier patrolling the outer defences; and a young deerhound.

BENHOLM'S LODGING AND THE FIDDLEHEAD

The area of the Castle overlooking the main entrance holds a few final surprises for the visitor.

The path skirting the north side of the Keep leads, via a short pend, to the top floor of Benholm's Lodging. (This can alternatively be reached via a staircase from the Inner Defences, which passes the 'Lion's Den' – a hollow dug out from the rock above the Gatehouse.)

Benholm's Lodging is named after James Keith of Benholm, a son of the 5th Earl Marischal, and may have been built for him. Designed in a rhomboid shape to fit an awkward location, it houses fearsome defences in its lower floors, guarding the Castle's main entrance.

By contrast, its upper floors would have made a comfortable dwelling for James Keith. The top floor now houses a small exhibition about the Castle's history and a scale model of the Castle. Among other exhibits are photographs of coins from various periods found in the Castle.

The rocky ridge overlooking the entrance to the Castle behind Benholm's Lodging is known as the Fiddlehead, perhaps because its curve resembles the scroll of a violin.

Below the present walkway, an arched doorway is visible, covered by an iron grille. This secondary entrance to the Castle is known as Wallace's Postern: it is said to be the gateway by which William Wallace entered the Castle to massacre an English army in 1297. However, there is no evidence of a castle existing here at that date and the story is almost certainly a myth. The postern has found a new role as a wishing well.

◗ Some of the artefacts (clay pipes, musket balls and a flint tool) found at the Castle, now on display in the top floor of Benholm's Lodging.

HISTORIC EVENTS AT DUNNOTTAR CASTLE

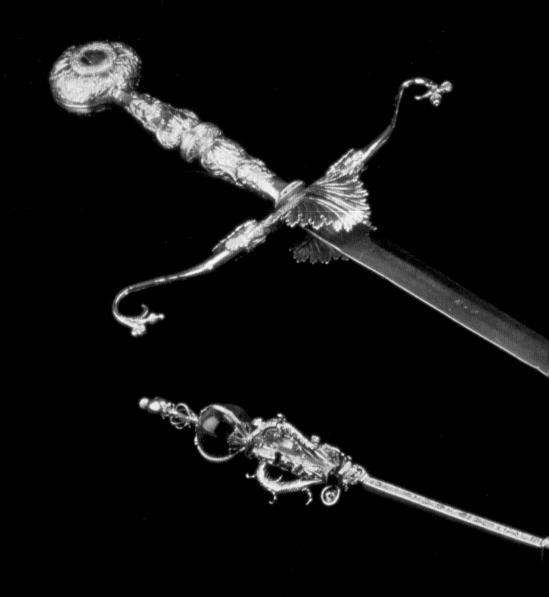

1297: WILLIAM WALLACE MASSACRES THE ENGLISH

In 1296, King Edward I of England invaded Scotland, beginning 60 years of struggle known as the Wars of Independence.

Edward made quick gains through the Borders, but met with guerrilla resistance, led by Sir William Wallace and Sir Andrew Moray. Famously, they defeated an English army at Stirling Bridge in September 1297.

Legend has it that Wallace trapped an English force, supposedly 4,000 strong, at Dunnottar, where they had fled seeking sanctuary. There is no evidence of a castle at that time, but the Chapel had been consecrated in 1276.

Wallace is alleged to have shown no mercy and set fire to the Chapel, condemning all inside to a terrible death. Others were driven over the cliff edges, with no survivors.

These events are recorded in Blind Harry's verse biography Wallace. Written nearly 200 years later, it is known more for enthusiasm than accuracy, however, the gist of the story may well be true.

○ William Wallace as depicted in stained glass at the National Wallace Monument in Stirling.

MARIE
REINE
DESCO...

© Victoria and Albert Museum, London

1562: MARY QUEEN OF SCOTS SEEKS RESPITE

In autumn 1562, Mary Queen of Scots, 19 years of age, faced her first major rebellion, led by the 4th Earl of Huntly, known as the Cock o' the North. The events came to a head on 28 October at the Battle of Corrichie, near Banchory, 15 miles (24km) north-west of Dunnottar Castle.

The youthful queen showed admirable resolve and her superior forces defeated the unruly Huntly, who died there and then of a seizure. His corpse was later taken to Edinburgh and convicted of treason.

Huntly's son Sir John, whose aim had been to kidnap the Queen and force her to marry him, was beheaded at Aberdeen on 2 November 1562. Mary was compelled to watch the execution, partly to refute any suggestion that she had encouraged him to woo her. This unpleasant spectacle was made more painful by Sir John's assertion on the scaffold that he was dying because of his love of her. Mary was reduced to tears by the ordeal.

It was a few days after this, on 5 and 6 November, that she stayed at Dunnottar Castle, where she was warmly welcomed by William Keith, 4th Earl Marischal.

This was not the only time Mary Queen of Scots stayed at Dunnottar. She returned some two years later, spending two nights in the Castle in September 1564.

● Coins found at the Castle, dating from the reign of Mary Queen of Scots (1542–67).

39

1645: MONTROSE LAYS WASTE TO STONEHAVEN

The dramatic events at Dunnottar Castle in the 1600s stemmed largely from the religious policies of King Charles I of Scotland, England and Ireland (reigned 1625–49).

The son of James VI, and the last king to be born in Scotland, Charles became convinced that the Scottish church should adopt episcopacy – government by bishops – like the English church.

Many Scots did not agree, and in 1638 signed the National Covenant, embracing Presbyterianism, a more democratic form of church governance. Charles' rejection of the Covenant led to armed rebellion which continued sporadically for half a century – including a grim episode at Dunnottar almost 50 years later (see pages 44–45).

● James Graham, 1st Marquess of Montrose.

● William Keith, 7th Earl Marischal.

In February 1639, William Keith, 7th Earl Marischal joined the Covenanters, then led by James Graham, Marquis of Montrose. In June that year, the Earl brought men and cannon to attack Royalist forces at nearby Megray Mill. Montrose requested that he keep Dunnottar Castle open in case of retreat, but this proved unnecessary. The Covenanters won at Megray and went on to take Aberdeen.

However, in the years that followed, Montrose switched allegiance, fearing the overthrow of the monarchy. He came to Dunnottar in 1645 at the head of a Royalist army and attempted negotiation with the Earl Marischal. The Earl repeatedly refused, ensconced in the Castle with a few supporters and 16 Presbyterian ministers.

When diplomacy failed, Montrose's vengeance was swift and savage. Stonehaven, Dunnottar and Fetteresso were plundered and burned, together with crops and vessels in the harbour. The Earl held fast in his Castle while his barony burned, comforted little by the assurance of the Presbyterian preacher Andrew Cant that, *'the reek will be a sweet-smelling savour in the nostrils of the Lord'*.

● A coin found at the Castle. It dates from around 1650, at the height of the Covenanting era.

● Stonehaven today.

1651: THE HONOURS OF SCOTLAND

Charles I's troubles did not end with the Covenanters. By the mid-1640s, Scotland, England and Ireland were plunged into civil war known as the War of the Three Nations.

In 1648, Charles I was arrested and tried for treason. In January 1649 he was beheaded by Parliament, which assumed control of Great Britain. Many Scots were appalled and turned to the king's eldest son Charles, then living in The Hague in the Netherlands. Within a week, he was declared King of Scotland in his absence.

The young King eventually arrived in Scotland in June 1650, aiming to recover his late father's kingdom, and made an

● The new King, Charles II.

uneasy truce with the Covenanters. On 8 July 1650 he was a guest of the 7th Earl Marischal at Dunnottar.

The young King's arrival prompted an invasion of Scotland by the Parliamentary Army led by Oliver Cromwell. After a failed attempt to take Edinburgh in July, Cromwell defeated a Scottish army at Dunbar and by Christmas had captured Edinburgh Castle.

It was at this time that the Earl Marischal fulfilled a duty bestowed on him by his title: to protect the Scottish crown jewels – crown, sword and sceptre – known as the Honours of Scotland. These magnificent emblems of the monarchy had been smuggled from Edinburgh Castle to Scone Abbey in Perthshire, where they were used for a hasty coronation of Charles II on 1 January 1651. From Scone, they were transported to Dunnottar, together with the King's papers and other valuables for safekeeping

Any sense of safety was undermined by the arrest soon afterwards of the Earl Marischal, who was imprisoned in the Tower of London. At this point, custody of Dunnottar Castle – and the Honours – fell to George Ogilvy of Barras, an experienced soldier and a trusted ally of the Earl.

● Oliver Cromwell.

1651–52: DEFENDING THE HONOURS

It was not long before Cromwell's men came to Dunnottar in pursuit of their prize.

In September 1651, Dunnottar Castle's guards saw what they must have feared for months: a detachment of Parliamentarian troops, known as 'Roundheads' encamped on the Black Hill, where the Stonehaven War Memorial now stands.

Initially, the Roundheads lacked the firepower to take the mighty Castle by force, but they could apply pressure to George Ogilvy and his garrison of 69 men. As winter set in, supplies soon ran short, and desperate missions had to be undertaken to gather food. The months went by and by May 1652, Cromwell's army had conquered the rest of Scotland. Dunnottar alone stood undefeated.

● George Ogilvy, defender of the Honours of Scotland at Dunnottar Castle.

That month the heavy artillery arrived. Ogilvy and his forces endured ten days of 'the havock of bombs and the shoaks of thundering Cannon', but by 24 May 1652 they had to surrender with full military honours.

However, despite the Roundheads' best efforts, the Honours had been saved. Secretly lowered down the side of the castle rock, they had been collected by a serving woman supposedly gathering seaweed on the beach – one of several extremely brave women who risked severe punishment to save the Honours.

They were then smuggled through the Parliamentarian lines by Anne Lindsay, a relation of Ogilvy's wife. The Honours were then taken in great secrecy to nearby Kinneff Church.

They were initially hidden by the minister, Rev James Grainger, and his wife Christian at the foot of their bed. Soon afterwards however, fearing for their safety the Graingers buried them under the flagstones of the church.

The Roundheads were furious and ransacked the Castle. Ogilvy and his wife were held prisoner there and brutally treated. He survived the ordeal, but cruelly she did not.

Meanwhile, the Graingers risked their lives looking after the Honours, digging them up periodically and drying them to prevent damage. They remained there until 1660, when Charles II was restored to the throne in England. Stone memorials in honour of Grainger and Ogilvy are displayed at Kinneff Church.

IN COMMEMORATION OF THE DEFENCE OF THE HONOURS OF SCOTLAND
FROM SEPTEMBER 1651 TO MAY 1652
BY GEORGE OGILVY OF BARRAS GOVERNOR OF DUNNOTTAR
AND OF THE HELP GIVEN BY HIS WIFE ELIZABETH DOUGLAS
AND BY HER KINSWOMAN ANNE LINDSAY

1685: MISTREATMENT OF THE WHIGS

After he was restored to the English throne in 1660, Charles II turned his back on his former allies the Covenanters.

In 1661, he imposed episcopacy – church rule by bishops – upon his Scottish subjects, who were mainly Presbyterian. The Covenanters however continued to practise the Presbyterian form of worship at secret meetings called conventicles.

As a display of their discontentment a group of nine Covenanters intercepted the Archbishop of St Andrews, James Sharp, in a carriage at Magus Moor near St Andrews in 1679. After shooting his guard, they assassinated the Archbishop with multiple stab wounds.

Enraged by this, and eager to stamp out Covenanting activity, Charles's government resorted to the imprisonment, torture and execution without trial of suspected Covenanters. This period was later known as 'The Killing Time'.

◐ The Whigs' Vault.

The situation came to a head following the death of Charles II in February 1685 and the succession of his Catholic brother, James VII of Scotland and II of England. The new Catholic King caused great anxiety to the Protestants who wanted Scotland and England to remain Protestant.

In May 1685, Archibald Campbell, 9th Earl of Argyll led a rebellion against King James. He was supported by the Covenanters, together with the Whigs, members of an anti-Catholic and anti-Royalist faction which eventually became a major political party.

When the government learned of this new threat, Covenanting prisoners from various parts of Scotland were brought to Edinburgh and ordered to swear allegiance to the King. Those who refused were brought to Dunnottar – remote from the anticipated fields of battle – to await penal transportation overseas. On 24 May 1685 they were imprisoned in the chamber now known as the Whigs' Vault.

The prisoners included 122 men, 45 women, and possibly some children. Of these 167 prisoners, 37 of them capitulated and signed an oath of allegiance to the King, while at least five died during the ordeal. Some 25 escaped, though 15 were recaptured and tortured, and two fell from the cliff face. After 10 weeks of misery, about 120 were dispatched on a penal ship to the West Indies, but as many as 70 died during the journey.

Aside from the memorial to the 'bairn of nyn years' in the Graveyard, the victims are commemorated on the Covenanters' Stone at Dunnottar Kirk yard, near Stonehaven.

● King Charles II in later life, after turning his back on the Covenanters.

'They had not the least accommodation for sitting, leaning or lying, and were perfectly stifled or want of air. They had no access to ease nature, and many of them were faint and sickly ... The barbarities of their keepers and soldiers were beyond expression.'

– Rev Robert Wodrow, The History of the Sufferings of the Church of Scotland (1721)

1715: THE 10TH EARL MARISCHAL FIGHTS FOR THE JACOBITES

In 1688, the Catholic King James VII was driven into exile by Protestant forces, led by William of Orange, Dutch husband of his Protestant daughter Mary. William and Mary then reigned jointly as William II (of Scotland) and III (of England) and Mary II.

○ George Keith, 10th Earl Marischal, who fought for the Jacobites.

The so-called 'Glorious Revolution', which ended the Catholic monarchy, was not universally supported. Followers of exiled King James became known as Jacobites (from Jacobus, the Latin form of James).

Their struggle to reinstate a Catholic Stuart dynasty to the throne began with the first Jacobite Rising of 1689. At this time George Keith, 8th Earl Marischal garrisoned Dunnottar Castle on behalf of William and Mary.

Later Earls Marischal, however, took up the Jacobite cause. William Keith, 9th Earl was imprisoned at Edinburgh Castle for Jacobitism in 1708. His son, George Keith, 10th Earl would prove an even more loyal Jacobite.

The Jacobite Rising of 1715 was prompted by the succession to the British throne of King George I. He was born in Hanover, a distant cousin of Queen Mary and her younger sister Queen Anne. Unlike the surviving Stuart line, he was Protestant.

The Jacobites naturally opposed the Hanoverian succession and believed the rightful heir to the British throne was Prince James Francis Stuart – the Catholic son of James VII. Known as the 'Old Pretender', he was living in exile in France.

At Braemar, in September 1715, the Earl of Mar declared James Stuart King and launched a military campaign to overthrow George I. He was joined by the 10th Earl Marischal, who drummed up support for the Pretender in north-east Scotland, supplying troops and cannon from Dunnottar.

The 10th Earl and his younger brother James Keith both fought at the crucial but indecisive Battle of Sheriffmuir in November 1715, and met the Pretender soon after he arrived in Scotland in December that year.

The Keith brothers accompanied Prince James in the weeks that followed, but the cause was lost almost before it began. On 30 January 1716, they escorted their would-be king to Montrose, where he boarded a ship for France, never to return.

As a result of the 10th Earl's gallant service to the Jacobite cause, he forfeited his estates, including Dunnottar Castle, which had been owned by the Keith family for over 400 years. It fell from use and by 1718, it was being dismantled, its roofs, floors and furnishings sold off to the highest bidder.

It was again owned by the Keith family from 1761 until 1873, but saw little use during this period.

◐ The East Range, seen from a window in the Marischal Suite.

◐ Prince James Francis Edward Stuart, the focus of the Jacobite movement.

49

DUNNOTTAR AS A VISITOR ATTRACTION

A few decades after Dunnottar's demise, it began to find a new lease of life.

◗ One of the Castle's earliest visitors' books, dating from 1894.

By the end of the 1700s, visiting ruined castles had become a fashionable pursuit. With its striking location and dramatic history, Dunnottar soon became a focus of interest. A romantic engraving of the Castle by James Sargant Storer, published in 1811, provides evidence of this growing trend.

By the 1880s, a visitors' book was in use at the Castle, and shows that people were willing to travel from as far as London and even Canada to explore the ruins.

In 1919, the Castle was purchased by Weetman Pearson, 1st Viscount Cowdray. He and his wife Annie set about restoring the Castle. The Castle remains in the Pearson family who continue to preserve and maintain it to this day.

Today, Dunnottar Castle is one of Scotland's most popular and spectacular attractions. It has featured in fashion shoots and films, including as inspiration for Disney/Pixar's Brave. Recent visitors' books demonstrate its world-class appeal, with visitors from as far afield as China and Japan, the USA and Brazil.

Maggie A. Howie	Auchinblae.
Lily A. Greig.	Auchinblae.
J. Anderson	Peterhead
M. Dickie	" "
John Cunningham	Glasgow
Sarah Sparrow Cunningham	Glasgow.
Lizzie P. Todd	Durris.
Geo. Todd	Durris
Mrs Wm. Gregory	Stonehaven
Wm. Gregory	"
James Burke, Solicitor,	Aberdeen.
Charles L. Keene	Aberdeen
Helen A. Methven	Edinburgh.
Jessie C. Mathven	Edinburgh
Janett MacDonald	Dufftown.
A. W. Hadden	São Paulo, Brazil
Photo E. Hadden	when the nuts come, from do
Maggie C. Hadden	Luthermuir
Edith Roose	London
Robson Roose	London
P. Sybil Robertson	Muchalls Castle
J. D. White IPS	"
Of F. E. Thorn.	Carlton House.
J. M. Taylor.	Stonehaven
N. R. Smith	Edinburgh
Miss H. Taylor.	~~Dundee~~ Broughty Ferry
Mr Arklay	Broughty Ferry
Ruth Taylor	Stonehaven.
Geo. A. Wisely	Macduff
Lizzie Mitchell	Aberdeen
Sophia Tocher	Stonehaven
E. Stewart	London
M. Thompson	Aberdeen
Wm. Atkins	Aberdeen

21

● Bottlenose dolphins seen near the Castle.

● Eider duck.

● Puffin.

VISITING WILDLIFE

Thanks to its location on a rugged outcrop in the North Sea, Dunnottar Castle offers many opportunities to wildlife spotters.

● Peregrine falcon.

● Stoat.

SEABIRDS

Two and half miles (4km) south of Dunnottar is the appropriately named Fowlsheugh ('heugh' means a steep cliff), where the Royal Society for the Protection of Birds maintains a colony for many species of seabird.

Puffins are readily recognised for their bright red beaks, and kittiwakes take their name from their distinctive call. Fulmars can be identified by their stiff-winged style of flight, gliding on air currents.

Guillemots are clumsy-looking birds on land, but very agile swimmers; razorbills are similar but more slender. They spend most of their lives at sea, returning to land in summer to breed.

Look out also for skua, shag, cormorant and eider duck.

OTHER BIRDS

Sometimes seen is the majestic peregrine falcon, which can fly at speeds of over 200mph (320kph), and uses this power to strike with lethal force, often killing its prey by impact alone.

SEA MAMMALS

Keep an eye out to sea to catch glimpses of grey seals, common seals and bottlenose dolphins, all of which inhabit the waters around the castle rock.

LAND MAMMALS

Perhaps the star residents of the Castle are the stoats – small, secretive and very agile members of the weasel family that have been sighted peering through gaps in the walls near the ticket kiosk and scampering through the Pends.

◔ Fulmars.

◔ Razorbill.

◔ Common seal.